THE CHANNEL FOUR BOOK OF

SUMO

LYALL WATSON

SIDGWICK & JACKSON

LONDON

First published in Great Britain
in 1989
by Sidgwick & Jackson Limited
1 Tavistock Chambers,
Bloomsbury Way
London WC1A 2SG

Designed by Hammond Hammond
Produced by Grub Street

The Channel Four series of Sumo is
made by Cheerleader Productions,
London, and produced by Mike Milne.

ISBN 0 283 99962 4

Typesetting by Chapterhouse Ltd,
Formby, L37 3PX
Printed by The Eagle Press plc

CONTENTS

INTRODUCTION

Sumo, as viewers in Britain now know, can be addictive. The colour and the texture, the style and ceremony, are satisfying in themselves. They give us a glimpse into a vanishing world of dignity and courtesy, a world inhabited by gentle giants whose lives are dedicated to a sport that is also a religious ritual.

But there is more to it than that. Sumo is also astonishingly subtle. There is as much intricacy, as much craft, technical skill and personal flair evident in each brief bout as you will find in a whole game of good cricket.

Producer Mike Milne and I have taken pains to bring out this depth of detail in our coverage of Sumo for Channel Four over the past three years. And we know from the response we receive from viewers throughout the British Isles that you are getting the message, and that you like what you see.

They are delighted in Japan. The wrestlers and the Sumo authorities know that, for the first time ever, there is now an audience outside Japan that understands and respects Sumo – and they are excited about bringing their art to you live, in the flesh, on sacred ground in a British arena. This is going to happen in October 1991 at London's Royal Albert Hall.

Between now and then we are going to bring you another new Sumo series every year, keeping track of the tide of powerful young wrestlers who are coming through to challenge the supremacy of Chiyonofuji – whose reign as one of the greatest champions in history is coming near its end.

It is an exciting time in Sumo and you have a ringside seat.

Lyan Watson.

1 ORIGINS · HOW DID IT BEGIN?

*S*hinto, or the way of the gods, is a set of beliefs which still govern much of ceremonial life in Japan. Festivals there often include ritual competitions such as horse racing, archery or a tug-of-war, whose results are used to decide which of two rivals should have the blessing of the gods on their endeavours. And from the beginning of Japanese history, the most popular of such systems of divination was a wrestling match.

The first recorded sumo bout took place in 23 BC. It was a serious matter. The winner was the sole survivor. But as the centuries passed, ritual sumo became more refined and by the 8th century AD, it was being performed regularly as a part of normal worship at popular shrines.

On 8 September each year at the Kamo Shrine in Kyoto, a priest still officiates over the 'Ceremony of the Crows', during which children take part in a series of ritual sumo matches. And on 9 September, at Oyamazumi Shrine on the island of Omishima, a priest on his own performs one-man sumo in which he wrestles with, and is always defeated by, an invisible deity.

Both of these ceremonies are formal acts of appeasement rather than trials of strength. They are a way of making contact between man and spirit. And much of this flavour persists in sumo today, which has become a sport with rich prizes, but still retains the character of a dance as well as a duel.

During the medieval period, Shrine sumo was replaced by a military version in which the same wrestling techniques were used in hand-to-hand combat during battle. This Samurai sumo was a forerunner to the later martial arts of jujitsu and kenjitsu. And by the 16th century, when the feudal system began to break down, it could sometimes be seen on street corners being performed for coins by masterless samurai or *ronin*. But in the 17th

and 18th centuries, sumo was organized on a professional basis until, under the patronage of the Emperors, it became the national sport of Japan.

It still is. Baseball may draw bigger crowds, but seats at the six annual sumo tournaments are hard to get and there is live television coverage of all major bouts on each of the 90 days of activity every year.

The top wrestlers are national celebrities with their own flourishing fan clubs, who cannot help but be conspicuous wherever they go. And in recent years this passion has spread abroad.

Channel 4 is the first however to bring sumo on an official and regular basis to a television audience outside Japan.

2 THE FIGHTERS · WHO DOES SUMO?

*I*n theory, anyone big enough and heavy enough to make the grade. The minimum height and weight requirements for entering sumo are 5 ft 7 in and 155 lbs (11 stone, 1) if you are under 18, and 5 ft 8 in and 165 lbs (11 stone, 11) if you are over 18 years old. And you must of course be male.

In practice, it is very rare for anyone but Japanese to take part. There are, at the moment, a handful of Samoan and Tongan wrestlers in the lower ranks and one gloriously exceptional Hawaiian – at 547 lbs (39 stone, 1) the heaviest sumo wrestler ever – in the top Division. But it is difficult for most foreigners to cope with the joint demands of language and the rigours of life as an apprentice in what is still very much a feudal system.

Sumo wrestlers (more properly called *sumotori* or *rikishi*) come in a wide variety of shapes, but by the time that they reach the upper ranks, their average weight is over 300 lbs (21 stone, 6) and, thanks to postwar changes in the Japanese diet, the present average height is around 6 ft tall.

There are no weight divisions in sumo. All *rikishi* are technically heavyweights and tend to be somewhat pear-shaped. The ideal weight distribution is one which concentrates as much flesh as possible around the hips and thighs, to provide a low centre of gravity.

The training is vigorous, so despite their great bulk, *rikishi* are astonishingly supple. One routine exercise involves sitting in a full split position with legs stretched out to the side, while pressing the chest and chin to the ground. And while the weight might seem ponderous in normal walking, the speed of a good wrestler off his mark has to be seen to be believed. Many of them are excellent and light-footed dancers.

3 THE DIVISIONS · HOW ARE THEY RANKED?

*T*here are roughly 800 wrestlers active in the sumo profession, of whom over 700 are ranked into one of six official Divisions:

SUMO DIVISIONS

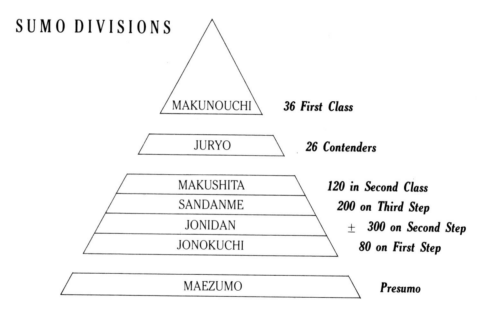

MAKUNOUCHI	*36 First Class*
JURYO	*26 Contenders*
MAKUSHITA	*120 in Second Class*
SANDANME	*200 on Third Step*
JONIDAN	*± 300 on Second Step*
JONOKUCHI	*80 on First Step*
MAEZUMO	*Presumo*

Beginners in the Presumo section are not official. They have no rights or privileges at all and must struggle to be recognized and included in the rankings.

The First Step up the pyramid brings a *rikishi* recognition, albeit only inclusion on the rankings in letters almost too small to be seen with the naked eye. And after that, he must earn promotion by consistently winning more bouts than he loses.

Rikishi of the lower ranks act as servants to senior wrestlers and coaches

— making their beds, doing their laundry, cooking, cleaning, running errands and carrying baggage.

But with promotion, life becomes a little easier. *Sandanme* wrestlers are relieved of the more tiresome chores. And once into the Second Class, all a *rikishi* is required to do is to supervise the beginners during their training periods. *Makushita* literally means 'below the curtain' and promotion from this Division into the top 62 changes everything.

The 36 First Class *rikishi* and the 26 Contenders are collectively known as *sekitori* and receive, for the first time, a monthly salary.

Juryo means ten *ryo* and refers to the top ten men amongst the Contenders, who in the old days received one *ryo* in currency as their wages. No *sekitori* is expected to do any work other than his own training and all get to bathe first, eat more and sleep later than those in lower ranks.

FIRST CLASS

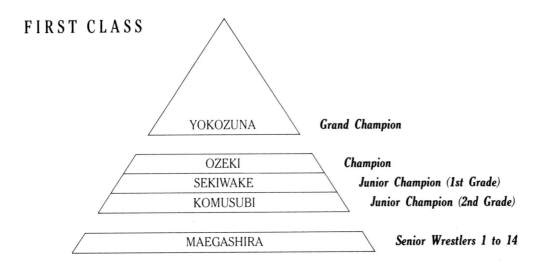

YOKOZUNA	*Grand Champion*
OZEKI	*Champion*
SEKIWAKE	*Junior Champion (1st Grade)*
KOMUSUBI	*Junior Champion (2nd Grade)*
MAEGASHIRA	*Senior Wrestlers 1 to 14*

'Inside the curtain' in the First Class or *Makunouchi* Division there is a further refinement of ranking.

At the bottom of the First Class are 24 to 28 fighters ranked as *Maegashira* numbers 1 to 14, with two men holding each rank.

Rikishi in this Division fight one of their own number on each day of a tournament and must score more wins than losses to get further promotion More losses than wins usually means automatic demotion.

Opposite: *Yokozuna* Chiyonofuji (right) congratulates Tagaryu on winning a tournament and getting his portrait onto the Wall of Fame.

Left: The *tsuna* or ceremonial belt worn by the supreme champion or *yokozuna*.

•

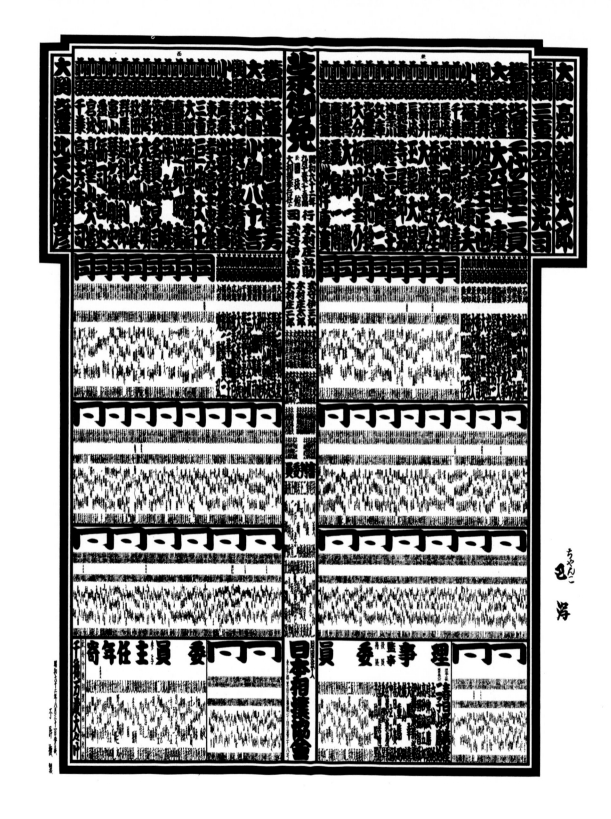

Above: Preparation of the *banzuke* by a traditional calligrapher, and opposite, the finished product.

•

Promotion from the top *Maegashira* position lifts a fighter into the three champion ranks known collectively as *sanyaku*. And this is where the real struggles begin.

Promotion to *komusubi* or Junior Champion (Grade 2) is a great honour. There are just two on this level, but it is always a difficult rank to maintain. In the first days of any tournament, the Junior Champions are traditionally matched against the big men above them and are often so demoralised by the time they get round to fighting lower ranks, that they lose these bouts too.

Promotion to the rank of *sekiwake* or Junior Champion (Grade 1) comes with consistently good performance in Grade 2, but moving up the next step is even harder. To make Champion, either of the two *sekiwake* must hold his rank for three consecutive tournaments with scores in double figures, which means at least ten wins out of fifteen. And this is something which only 1 in 500 *rikishi* ever achieve.

Ozeki means 'the great barrier'. There may be as many as six *rikishi* on this rank at one time and to break through to become Grand Champion or *yokozuna* is very rare and the ultimate honour in sumo. There have only been 62 *yokozuna*, ever.

Only a Champion who has performed extremely well on a consistent basis, and who has the right attitude, can ever hope to make the final grade. But once there, he can never be demoted. *Yokozuna* are beyond challenge. They are expected, however, to behave with honour. If a Grand Champion performs badly in a tournament, he usually drops out for 'health reasons'. And if his losing streak lasts too long, he is bound to retire altogether.

A ranking wrestler in a ceremonial apron.

•

There have been times when sumo has as many as four *yokozuna* in action and rare times when there are none. But sumo without a Grand Champion at all is in a very sad state.

With the exception of *yokozuna*, all wrestlers rise and fall through the ranks according to their most recent performance. There are usually no draws in sumo and with each of the *sekitori* fighting on every day of a 15-day tournament, there are no even scores. Therefore a record of more wins than losses means 8–7 or better — which is called *kachi-koshi*. While

Opposite: The *banzuke* or list of ranks for a tournament on display outside the stadium.

•

a majority of losses means 7–8 or worse — which is known as *make-koshi*.

A perfect score is 15–0 (known as *zensho-yusho*) and guarantees victory. More often, a tournament winner has a record of 14–1 or 13–2. Any score in double figures is considered good and earns promotion for all but *ozeki*, who have to be even more conspicuously successful. But, as a rule, 10–5 or 9–6 is good enough to carry a middle-ranking *rikishi* a couple of rungs up the ladder, while 8–7 brings only a slight promotion. Records of 7–8 mean one step down the ranks, once again with the exception of *ozeki*, who have to score 7–8 or lower in at least two consecutive *basho* to be punished by a fall to lower ranks.

All rankings are decided by the ruling body of sumo. Their decisions are written in traditional calligraphy on a large board called a *banzuke*, which is photographed and published 13 days before the start of each new *basho*. On the very bottom line of every *banzuke* there appears the traditional wish —

'May sumo continue to draw full audiences yet another thousand and ten thousand years.'

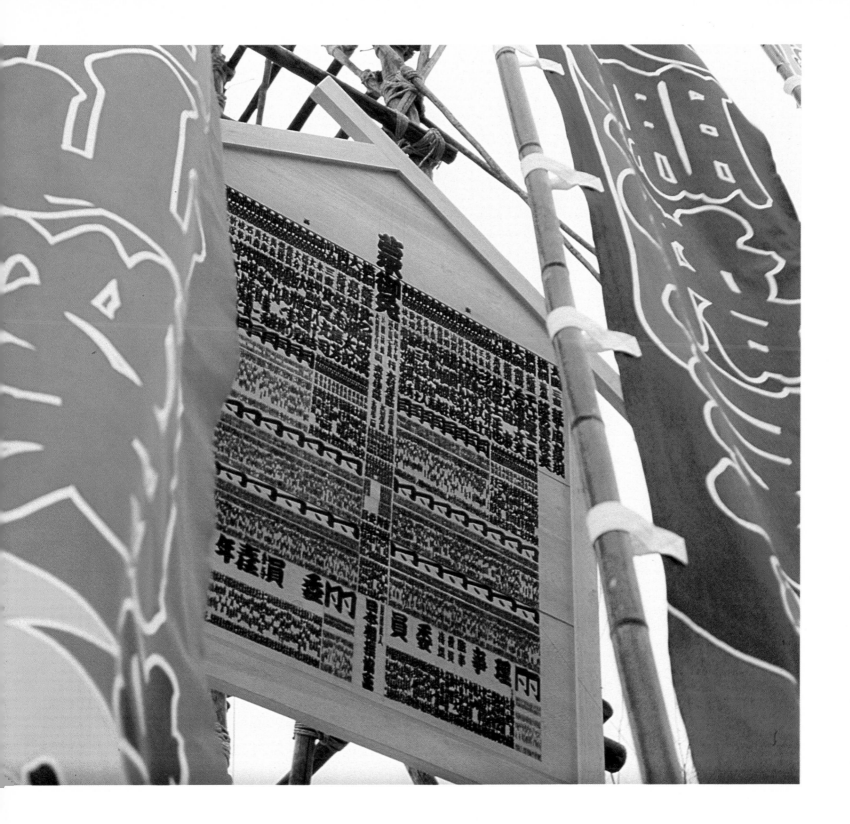

4 DRESS · WHAT DO THEY WEAR?

*T*here is something about the size and bearing of a sumo champion that is unmistakeable, even in the traditional Japanese kimono that every *rikishi* wears at all times in public. But the best way of identifying any wrestler, even in the dark, is by his distinctive smell.

All *rikishi* oil their hair with *bintsuke*, a pomade scented with camellia, that holds it firmly in place during bouts. Hair is grown long and those in the lower ranks always fasten theirs in a simple topknot or *chon-mage*. Wrestlers in the top two Divisions are allowed to wear theirs in a style known as *o-icho-mage*, in which the hair is pulled back, tied and then doubled forward in a fan which is shaped like the leaf of the sacred *ginkgo* tree.

Young *rikishi* may do each other's hair, but the *sekitori* always enjoy the services of a fulltime sumo hairdresser or *tokoyama*, who comes equipped with a traditional set of boxwood combs.

Sumo wrestlers in action wear a belt or loincloth known as a *mawashi*. This is over 10 yds of material, folded lengthwise four or six times, wrapped around the waist, passed between the legs and tied in the back with a knot. Those worn in the lower four Divisions are always of black canvas — often faded with long use to grey. While the upper two Divisions practise in white canvas cloths and fight in *mawashi* of pure silk in a variety of colours. Traditionalists prefer black, but red, purple, green, gold and blue are becoming increasingly popular.

During tournament bouts, *sekitori* also wear a thin belt tucked into the bottom of the loincloth. This is the *sagari*, which is patterned after the sacred ropes that dangle from *Shinto* shrines, and has 19 starched silk threads hanging from it. Some *rikishi* prefer 17 or 21 threads, but the number is always uneven and the belt itself has no practical function, often

Opposite
Left: The average weight of top wrestlers is well over twenty stone, but these big men are surprisingly light on their feet.
Right: Three stages in a *tokoyama* **or sumo barber's daily task of oiling, shaping and tying of a wrestler's hairstyle.**

•

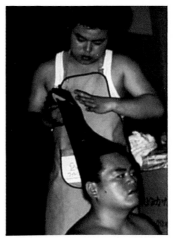

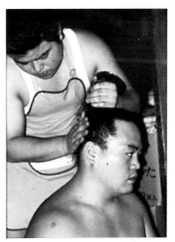

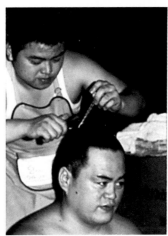

Maenoshin wearing an ornamental apron bearing his name on the left and that of his patron at the bottom.

•

Wrestlers of the top division in their *kesho-mawashi*.

falling off during a bout or being ripped loose immediately afterwards.

At the start of bouts in their Divisions, *juryo* and *makunouchi* wrestlers also take part in a ceremony during which they wear coloured aprons or *kesho-mawashi*. These hang down in the front to ankle length. They are handwoven silk, always highly decorated with gold and silver brocade and sometimes with pearls or other precious stones. Even an ordinary one costs around £4,000, but some of the more spectacular ones are valued at over £20,000 — and popular *rikishi* may have one for every day of a tournament.

Kesho-mawashi bear pictures or Japanese calligraphy and often carry the name of the owner and, at the bottom, just above the fringe, the name of the sponsor or fan club responsible for donating the precious garment.

5 ORGANIZATION · WHO RUNS SUMO?

Opposite: The top officials of the Sumo Association pay their respects to the Shinto gods before a tournament and, above, at the opening of the new Kokugikan stadium in Tokyo.

•

*I*n the early days, sumo was organized by several separate bodies in Tokyo, Osaka and Nagoya. But since 1927, responsibility has been in the hands of a joint body which in 1958 was renamed the Japan Sumo Association — Nihon Sumo Kyokai.

The Association consists today of the active wrestlers and officials together with 105 elders divided into committees which supervise every aspect of professional sumo. Each of the 105 elders bears a traditional hereditary name which he must buy from the Association.

In theory, each of these elders has the right to set up a *heya* or stable in which the *rikishi* live and train. But at the moment there are just 39 stables, each led by an ex-wrestler who has become an *oyakata* or master by arranging the transfer of stock from an elder reaching the mandatory retiring age of 65. Since salaries and benefits go with being an elder, the name is expensive and difficult to obtain — and seldom changes hands these days for much less than £400,000.

So 39 stable-masters and 66 (at the moment an exceptional 68) other elders together run an organization headed by ten of their number on a board of directors. And it is these men who control the finances, subsidize the stables, organize the tournaments, rank the wrestlers and keep a watchful and conservative eye on sumo, ensuring that its traditions remain intact.

It is this body, the Japan Sumo Association, that has given express permission for Channel 4 television to produce the first programmes of sumo coverage specifically intended for a non-Japanese audience.

6 THE RING · WHERE DOES SUMO TAKE PLACE?

*I*n practice or in earnest, sumo takes place on a ring called the *dohyo*. This is a hard clay platform, 18 ft square. In its centre is a circle of 20 small rice straw bales sunk into the clay to form a ring just under 15 ft in diameter. One bale is removed from each of the four cardinal compass directions and set slightly outside the circle. The original reason for this was to allow rainwater to drain from outdoor rings, but the arrangement has been retained indoors, giving the fighters a few extra inches of space to play with at these crucial points.

Beyond the fighting circle lies a square marked off by a further 32 bales. And access to the tournament *dohyo*, which is raised roughly 30 inches from the stadium floor, is simplified by nine sets of straw-fringed steps cut into the clay.

Building such a *dohyo* takes three days, requires seven truck loads of special clay and involves elaborate ritual supervised by a *shinto* priest and ending with the ring ceremony or *dohyo matsuri* on the day before each tournament. For this, three referees robed in white consecrate wooden sticks representing the four seasons with the words — 'Long life to earth and may the wind and rain faithfully follow'.

One of the sticks, decorated with folded strips of white paper attractive to the gods of creation, is placed in each corner of the *dohyo*. And an unglazed earthenware pot, filled with good luck charms such as dried chestnuts, seaweed and cuttlefish, is buried in the centre of the ring with offerings of salt and *sake*.

Directly above the *dohyo* is a wooden roof in the style of a *Shinto* shrine. This used to be supported by four wooden pillars, but to provide

Above: Some of the paraphernalia of Sumo — cedar waterbucket, tissues, wooden clappers and brooms between bouts.
Opposite
Above left: Seven truckloads of special clay are sculpted into the platform of the *dohyo*.
Above right: Rice straw is shaped into bales that are let into the surface of the ring.
Below: The finished *dohyo*, complete with steps, spitoons and platforms for salt and water.

29

Above: The shrine canopy which hangs over the ring, with coloured silk tassles representing the four seasons.
Left: *Gyoji* pouring a *sake* offering onto the ring during the dedication ceremony.
Opposite: Shinto priests purify the *dohyo* before the opening of the new Kokugikan stadium.

•

Above: A referee in the costume of a Shinto priest in the ring dedication ceremony that precedes each tournament.
Opposite: Tokyo's Kokugikan, the home of sumo.

•

better visibility it is now suspended by cables from the ceiling. The pillars have been replaced by silk tassles in the colours of the four seasons — green for spring (to the east), red for summer (to the south), white for autumn (to the west) and black for winter (to the north). Woven bamboo baskets of salt are placed beneath the red and white corners, together with cedar buckets of water for use in purification rituals.

The four colours and directions are based on the *I Ching*, and together with the inner ring represent the five elements and the five virtues of Confucianism. The rice straw circle symbolises the ritual of harvest around the ring itself — 'the realm of the absolute.'

In Tokyo's new stadium, Kokugikan, a basic clay platform is kept between tournaments beneath the stadium floor and rises on a lift for completion and dedication on the days before a *basho*. When it is completed a thin layer of sand is added as a symbol of purity. It is nevertheless, and at all times, regarded as sacred ground, never to be touched by shoes or, under any circumstances, by a woman.

During a tournament, the *dohyo* is maintained by the *yobidashi* or sumo announcers, who sweep the circle of sand immediately outside the ring of bales so that footmarks will show when a wrestler is forced out. And, approximately every hour, when the team of judges is changed, several *yobidashi* come on and sprinkle the entire *dohyo* surface with just enough water to provide a firm footing.

7 THE BASHO · WHAT HAPPENS AT A TOURNAMENT?

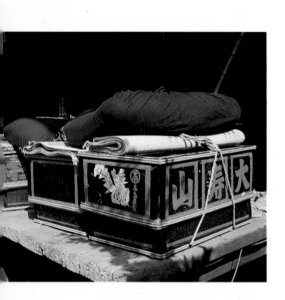

Above: Akeni, the wicker baskets in which wrestlers keep their ceremonial aprons.
Opposite: Supreme Champion Chiyonofuji performing his *dohyo-iri* or ring-entering ceremony flanked by two assistants known as 'the sword-bearer' and 'the dew-sweeper'.

•

*S*umo tournaments are, rather appropriately, known as *basho*. There are six a year at two-monthly intervals:

January	Hatsu Basho	The First Tournament in Tokyo
March	Haru Basho	The Spring Tournament in Osaka
May	Natsu Basho	The Summer Tournament in Tokyo
July	Nagoya Basho	The Fourth Tournament in Nagoya
September	Aki Basho	The Fall Tournament in Tokyo
November	Kyushu Basho	The Last Tournament in Fukuoka

Tickets go on sale six weeks before a tournament at prices ranging from £4 a day for unreserved seats at the back, to £40 for a ringside cushion. Access to all the best seats is controlled by 20 traditional sumo teashops or *chaya*, each of which has exclusive rights to a hundred or more *masuzeki* — *tatami* matted boxes holding four people sitting Japanese style in what we would call the stalls.

Boxes are rented for long periods by companies or rich patrons and are almost impossible to obtain on a casual basis. If one is available, it is likely to cost about £150 a day. Food and drink, which is on liberal supply from the ushers of the teashops, is extra. Inviting three guests to join you in your box for one day of sumo with all the trimmings could easily set you back £400. But the majority of sumo enthusiasts make do with an ordinary seat in the circle at about £15 and an occasional beer or *sake*.

Sumo crowds are highly vocal, calling out the names of their favourites or shouting '*Ganbare*! Go for it!' or a more derisive '*Makeru zo*! Forget it,

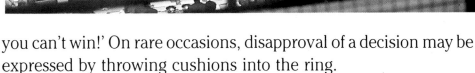

you can't win!' On rare occasions, disapproval of a decision may be expressed by throwing cushions into the ring.

Tournaments all last 15 days which, with the exception of the first and last, begin early in the morning with new recruits trying to earn a place in the lowest Division. They perform with few formalities in front of an almost empty hall and after each bout the winner stays in the ring to face a second opponent. If he wins again, he receives a 'white star'. Four such stars in a tournament will put him in the rankings of the *jonokuchi* next time.

So for the first few hours of each day, a long succession of lower-ranking *rikishi* do battle with each other almost without pause under the eyes of teenage officials. Until finally, in mid afternoon, the television lights go on and the real contenders appear.

Each pair of fighters is announced from the ring by a *yobidashi*, who sings out their names over his fan in a traditional manner which makes them almost incomprehensible. These are the same officials who sweep the ring between bouts and who bring on the banners which

Above: An announcer or *yobidashi* sings out the names of the fighters about to take the ring.
Above left: Seating close to the ring occupied by judges, favoured patrons on the cushions in the first six rows and enthusiasts in the four-cushion boxes that fill the stalls.
Opposite: Senior *gyoji* announcing the draw for the following day's bouts.

•

The high *shiko* stamp of a *yokozuna*.

make a circuit of the *dohyo* before an important match, announcing the names of sponsors who have put up a prize.

All *sekitori* in the upper Divisions fight 15 times during a tournament, never meeting the same opponent twice, unless there is a tie for first place on the last day.

The pairings for all bouts are made up by a committee of judges 2 days in advance. These are decided both on rank and on performance in a tournament. The champions meet with challengers down to about mid-level in their Division during the first week and then clash with fellow champions in the last few days. The sequence, however, is flexible and if a low-ranked fighter is performing brilliantly, he may well be matched with a Champion or even a Grand Champion in a pairing which crowds are likely to find pleasing. Everyone enjoys seeing one of the great men overturned against all the odds.

Days on which the Emperor himself is in the audience are special, but excitement builds every day as bouts are televised from about 4 pm — and things reach a climax just before 6 pm when the *yokozuna* have their matches.

The last day of a tournament is known as *senshuraku* and if two *rikishi* are on the same score and likely to be involved in a play-off for the championship, a sell-out is guaranteed. Then, four white banners unfurl from the ceiling above the ring displaying the characters *man'in onrei* — 'Full House Thank You'.

Above: The banners above the ring which announce a 'Full House'.
Opposite: Supreme Champion Chiyonofuji with attendants after performing his *dohyo-iri* at Ise Shrine.

8 CEREMONY · WHAT DO THE RITUALS MEAN?

Wrestlers in the top two divisions are divided, purely for the sake of symmetry, into teams who enter from east and west. Traditionally, the men on the eastern side rank slightly above their equivalents to the west. And just before the *sekitori* matches begin at about 3 pm, the *juryo* men arrive on the arena in single file dressed in their colourful *kesho-mawashi*. Each mounts the *dohyo* as his name is called and all then turn to face the crowd and perform a brief routine in which they clap once, give their aprons a jaunty hitch and raise one hand before filing out again to change into their regular loincloths.

This ring-entering ceremony dates back to the 17th century and, like much else in sumo, has *Shinto* overtones. Clapping is a ritual performed in front of all shrines to attract attention and to indicate the presence of one whose soul is pure. Lifting the apron is the ritualized version of a more robust gesture usually made to drive out devils. And arms are raised to show that the wrestlers, once recruits from the ranks of the samurai, are not concealing any weapons.

The *dohyo-iri* or ring-entering ceremony of the *yokozuna* is far more elaborate. It takes place after the other *rikishi* have announced themselves and involves not only the Grand Champion but two attendants who come marching down the aisle before and behind him. In front is the *tsuyu harai* or 'dew sweeper' who acts as a herald, and behind strides the *tachi mochi* or 'sword bearer' who serves as a bodyguard.

The *yokozuna* himself wears a snow-white belt of thick hemp rope tied behind him in a sweeping bow. This hawser or *tsuna* weighs as much as 32 lbs and is the symbol of a Grand Champion's authority. From it hang the

Above: The traditional forms of *tsuna* belt worn by all *yokozuna*. Opposite: The referee supervises *shikiri-naoshi*, the essential preliminaries that provide sumo's fascinating 'war of nerves'.

•

Above: The ring-entering ceremony of fighters in the top two divisions, clad in decorative *kesho-mawashi* or ceremonial aprons.

Left: *Yokozuna* wearing *tsuna* with dangling paper *gohei* during his ring-entering ceremony.

Opposite: *Yokozuna* stamping to drive evil spirits from the ring.

•

Opposite: Chiyonofuji, 'the Wolf', glares at his opponent during shikiri naoshi.

•

traditional *Shinto* zigzags of folded paper. The great man takes his position, squatting at the edge of the ring, flanked by his two attendants. He produces two resounding claps, rubbing his hands before him at arm's length in a symbolic purification with blades of grass that once preceded battle. Then he strides to the centre of the *dohyo*, turns to face north toward the Emperor (and the TV cameras) and claps once more.

Then comes the moment everyone has been waiting for. The *yokozuna* puts his left hand to his heart, extends his right arm out to the east and, raising his right leg as high as he can, brings it slamming down into the clay.

This is the *shiko*, a gesture that both frightens evil spirits out of the ring and expresses a fighter's intention of trampling his opponent into the dust. The crowd loves it and greets the stamp with a roar of approval that grows louder still as he repeats the ritual with his other leg, before bowing and leaving the ring. Then the first division matches begin.

Few bouts last more than ten action-filled seconds, but each is preceded by a fascinating round of ritual preliminaries. After entering the ring, the wrestlers throw salt (to purify the proceedings); warm up with one or two *shiko* stamps (to drive out any stray devils); squat; clap (to attract the attention of the gods); turn their palms up (to show that they are unarmed); wipe their bodies with tissues (for further purification); rinse their mouths with water (more ritual cleansing); spit with phenomenal accuracy into a pail; throw a bit more salt, perhaps licking some off their fingers (to sharpen their senses); and then crouch down on their marks and glare at each other.

This is *shikiri naoshi* — the heart and the most interesting part of sumo. It goes on for a maximum of three minutes before *juryo* matches and four minutes before *makunouchi* bouts. In the days before television, there was no time limit at all. What it still amounts to is psychological war. It is ritualized aggression in its purest form, involving prolonged eye contact and threatening postures, all designed to undermine an opponent's self-confidence and bolster one's own. It is so expressive that sumo enthusiasts and experienced students of behaviour can often tell, even before the *rikishi* come to actual grips with each other, who is likely to win.

Gyoji **controlling the**
preliminaries before a bout.

•

At the end of the ritual confrontation comes the moment of truth — the *tachi-ai*. As with so much else in sumo, nothing is written about this in the rules, but it is understood that before they charge, both wrestlers must touch the clay with both of their hands. *Tachi* means 'standing', but the suffix is a complex one that has to do with propriety and harmony, and the combination requires that the fighters do things properly, standing up together for a clean start.

The referee indicates, by turning the broad face of his fan towards the wrestlers, when it is time to go. But only the fighters themselves can decide when to actually begin, often prolonging the moment, perhaps even attempting to disconcert an opponent with a false start. All the best bouts, however, begin with the rivals simultaneously closing their own circuits, making co-ordinated contact with the clay and springing out together to meet at a precise mid-point in the fabric of space between them.

The great beauty of sumo is that, despite this elemental confrontation, the behaviour of *rikishi* on the *dohyo* is always very proper, filled with dignity and courtesy, and totally devoid of the juvenile antics that form such a large part of professional wrestling displays.

Perhaps the most vital ingredient in sumo ritual is salt. At the end of each training session in every stable, the *dohyo* is swept clean and three handfuls of salt are thrown across it, left, right and centre — leaving solemn, ghostly lines. Before leaving the stable for a match, wrestlers often take a handful of salt and sprinkle it over their feet, so that they start out clean. And even those who ignore such precautions are purified by passing between two little conical piles of salt on either side of the stable door.

At the tournament itself, salt consumption is so conspicuous that the Japan Sumo Association gets through over 100 lbs a day. Referees and announcers going in to work put a few grains on their tongues, to sanctify their words and decisions. And every wrestler in the top two Divisions decorates his preliminaries in the ring with several hefty throws, each of which is watched very carefully by his opponent and the crowd for clues to his state of mind. The more salt a man uses, the more nervous he is said to be; but some are just naturally flamboyant and the more canny ones are not above pretending to be nervous when they are not.

Two heavyweights in their
pre-fight configuration.

•

9 THE RULES · WHO WINS?

*T*he rules are very simple.

It is forbidden to punch with a closed fist, poke eyes, pull hair, kick an opponent in the stomach, choke him or grab that part of the loincloth that covers his genitals. Anything else goes. And the loser is the first fighter to leave the ring or to touch the ground, inside or outside the circle, with any part of his body except the soles of his feet.

The action is controlled by a *gyoji* or referee who wears a long robe, a medieval court hat and carries a fan. He signals with his broad fan when a bout should begin, and encourages the *rikishi* on to greater efforts by a continuous stream of '*Nokotta, nokotta!*' calls which mean nothing more than 'Hang in there!' Should the action stall, he changes his cry to '*Hakkeyoi!*', urging them to 'Keep going!' until the deadlock is broken.

It is the *gyoji* who decides who wins a bout, pointing with his fan to the east or west. And no *rikishi* ever questions such a decision. The judges however may do so. There are five of them, all elders or ex-Champions, seated on plump cushions at the centre of each side of the *dohyo* — with an extra man on the south to keep an eye on the time. On occasion, one or more will dispute a call by raising his hand. Then all the judges climb onto the *dohyo* and talk it over amongst themselves. The head judge, he who sits on the north side, wears an earphone connected to two further judges who watch a video replay of the action. Together, they reach a decision which may overturn that of the referee or call for an immediate rematch.

If a referee's call is judged to have been wrong, he gets a 'black star'. And two such penalties in a single tournament result in a lowering of rank. Which means a change of footwear and going back to referee bouts in a more junior division.

After a decision, both *rikishi* bow to the referee and the winner squats

Left: All five judges gather on the *dohyo* to discuss a decision.
Opposite: A senior *gyoji* or referee in traditional court costume and carrying his ceremonial fan.
Below: Two decorative *gunbai*, the referees' fans.

Above: *Yobidashi* announcing a bout.
Right: The prizegiving ceremony in which the referee hands the winner of the bout an envelope containing a cash reward, which he acknowledges with a slicing motion of his right hand.
Opposite: *Yumitori shiki* — the bow ceremony which brings each day's activities during a tournament to a ritual close.

on his side of the *dohyo* to receive his rewards. These usually consist of cash prizes donated by sponsors and presented in envelopes carried across by the referee on the flat side of his fan. The *rikishi* makes a quick gesture over these, chopping with his open hand to the left, to the right and to the centre of the envelopes (giving thanks to heaven, earth and man in turn) before walking off with the prize.

But before he can leave the arena, the winner must wait at the corner of the *dohyo* to offer a ladle of water, and a share of his good fortune, to the next wrestler on his team.

And after the last match of the day, a senior *rikishi* comes out to perform the *yumitori shiki*. This is a brief but very graceful twirling routine with a long bow. A reminder of a time when the winning wrestler at court tournaments was presented, not with money, but with a new bow to use in the defence of his warlord and master.

10 TECHNIQUES · HOW DO THEY WIN?

*T*here are said to be over 200 ways of winning a match in sumo. But in practice only 48 *kimarite* or techniques are regarded as common and less than half of these are seen with any frequency.

Broadly speaking, these techniques can be divided into two general categories:–

Oshi-Zumo   — 'pushing' or thrusting, and

Yotsu-Zumo — 'holding' or pulling techniques.

Traditionalists and knowledgeable sumo fans prefer the *yotsu* techniques — which depend upon one fighter getting a hold on the other's belt and either throwing him down inside the ring, or manoeuvering him to the edge of the circle and forcing, lifting or throwing him out. But in recent years more and more bouts have been won by some form of *oshi* — in which the fighters never come to grips at all.

The most common and, to western watchers the most surprising, *oshi* technique is simple 'open handed slapping' or *tsuppari*. In this, both hands are used rapidly and alternately to hit an opponent's chest or throat and blast him out of the ring.

A win by this method is called 'thrust down' (*tsuki taoshi*) if the opponent goes down inside the ring, and 'thrust out' (*tsuki dashi*) if he is pushed over the line.

The slapping technique is most often seen at the very beginning of a match, immediately following the *tachi-ai* or charge which brings the

Opposite: Asahifuji lifts Sakahoko out by *tsuri dashi* technique.

Tsuki dashi

Hataki komi

Hikkake

fighters into dramatic contact with each other. It can end a fight in seconds. Or it can lead to disaster if the opponent is quick enough to sidestep the charge and himself slap the attacker down while he is off balance. This is the 'slap down' or *hataki komi*.

Or, an opponent can move to the side of the arm making the first slap, grab it and pull his attacker off balance. This is the 'pull' *hikkake*.

An even more ignominious counter is the one used by some of the faster and lighter fighters. This is the 'dodge' *okuri dashi* and involves getting behind a slap-happy attacker and simply pushing him out of the ring.

A more considered *oshi* technique is to push rather than slap. This is done with the palm open and thumb and forefinger spread wide against the chin, throat or armpit of an opponent. A win by this method is a 'push out' or *oshi dashi*.

And if the loser goes down inside the ring, he succumbs to the 'push down' or *oshi taoshi*.

Another non-contact manoeuvre is the simple 'sweep' or *ketaguri* in which an opponent has his legs kicked out from under him as he charges.

But the real crowd-pleasers are the *yotsu* techniques.

The goal in these is to get your strongest arm inside your opponent's and grab him by the belt. Right arm under in a clinch is known as *migi yotsu* and left arm under as an *hidari yotsu* hold. Both arms on the inside and fixed to the belt is the very advantageous *moro zashi*.

In grapples of this kind, the heaviest wrestler has a distinct advantage and usually wins, most often by *yorikiri*, which is the 'force out', in which an opponent is simply marched out of the ring. In a recent survey of 3,261 bouts, a third were found to be won this way.

If the losing wrestler falls as he goes out, it is called *yori taoshi* or 'forcing out and down'.

A more dramatic conclusion to a bout involving a good solid grip on the belt is the 'lift out' or *tsuri dashi*.

One of the few exceptions to the rule that the wrestler who first touches the ground outside the ring loses, is the 'carry out' or *okuri ashi* in which a

Okuri dashi

Oshi dashi

The charge — two wrestlers leap out for the initial clash.

·

Yorikiri

Tsuri dashi

Right: *Chiyonofuji* throws
Kotogaume down inside the ring
by *uwatedashinage* technique.
Opposite: *Tsuki otoshi* technique
— an outer-arm belt throw.

·

Tsuki otoshi

Uchi-gake

Soto-gake

Kote nage

fighter holding an opponent aloft, as long as he is moving forward, can step beyond the rope himself and win.

Another variation of the 'lift out' is the 'lift down' or *tsuri otoshi* in which the wrestler with the good belt hold lifts an opponent and then forces him down to his knees.

The most simple defence against an opponent who has a good grip on your belt is to use your own weight to push him off balance to the ground. This is the 'push over' or *tsuki otoshi*.

When both fighters have good holds on each other's belts, the 'leg' techniques come into play.

Uchi-gake is the 'inner leg trip', which is done by wrapping your leg around an opponent from the inside.

Soto-gake is the 'outer leg trip'.

But the classic response to any impasse, with or without a good grip, is one of the sweeping 'hip throws' or *nage* techniques.

Shitate nage

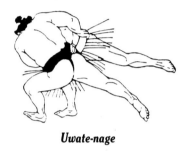

Uwate-nage

Kote nage is the 'forearm throw'. It is done by grasping an opponent's arm inside yours and twisting your hip at the same time as you bend forward and pull him down.

Shitate-nage, the 'inner-arm throw', is the variation most commonly used when your arm is inside that of your opponent.

Uwate-nage is the 'outer arm throw'. This is carried out by a similar manoeuvre, but with your arm not only outside, but firmly attached to your opponent's belt.

Sukui-nage the 'scooping throw', uses an arm around an opponent's shoulder.

And *kubi-nage*, the 'neck throw', is the variation in which you grasp him by the neck.

But perhaps the most stunning technique of all, one which always rouses the crowd, is called *utchari*. This is translated as 'throwing down at the edge of the ring'. It requires impeccable timing and only takes place when a wrestler finds himself at the edge of the ring and on the point of being forced out. Then, if he is quick and strong, he can bend back, lift his opponent off the ground and twist so that both fighters crash to the ground outside the ring with the initiator of the manoeuvre on top.

These 24 techniques are just half of those regarded as part of a wrestler's normal repertoire, but they represent well over 90 per cent of all throws likely to be seen in any tournament.

Most bouts last ten seconds or less, with the winner pushing the loser out very quickly or getting a grip on his belt that forces him to the ground. But where the initial charge fails to give either fighter an advantage, then manoeuvering for position may go on for a minute or more, until one or other of the wrestlers succeeds in catching the other off guard or off balance.

Weight counts for a lot in sumo, but timing is everything.

Sukui-nage

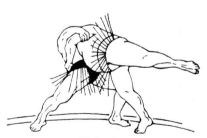

Utchari

11 PRIZES · HOW MUCH DO THEY EARN?

*H*ard to say, because sumo is the only sport in the world where the majority of those who earn their living from it, never see a pay cheque.

Only the *sekitori* of the top two divisions (62 out of more than 700) receive a monthly salary. This ranges from £1,600 for a *juryo* wrestler to £3,500 for a *yokozuna*.

All other *rikishi* receive only room and board, plus an allowance for each tournament in which they take part. This ranges from £250 for a trainee on the first step, to about £375 for a wrestler just below the truly professional curtain in the *makushita* division.

In addition, there is an elaborate system of incentives. When a young wrestler appears on the *banzuke* for the first time, he is credited with three yen. And every time he comes out of a tournament with more wins than losses, this amount increases. Until, by the time most *rikishi* reach *juryo* level, they have a credit of about 30 or 40 yen. But he gets paid none of this unless he does reach the *juryo* division. And then the bonus figure is automatically multiplied by 1,500 — and this amount is paid to him after every tournament in which he does take part.

On top of that, every time a wrestler in the top division wins a championship or one of the performance prizes, a further increment of 50 yen is added to his bonus. This may not sound much, but it multiplies out to around £300 a *basho* for as long as the fighter is active. Old-timers, who may have accumulated as much as 1,000 yen points in a successful career, receive an automatic bonus of £5,000 to £6,000 for any tournament in which they remain in the top division, regardless of their performance. But

Opposite: The reward — Chiyonofuji holds the Emperor's Cup while his supporters celebrate with a shout of 'Banzai'.

it is rare for any fighter to remain active beyond the age of 35.

As well as salary and bonus money, known as *okome* or 'rice' in sumo slang, there are supplements of around £250 for each Tokyo tournament and travel allowances for provincial tours.

Actual prizes at each tournament range from about £80 for an ordinary bout (after the Association has deducted a percentage for pension and taxes), to over £10,000 for the Championship.

In addition to the Emperor's Cup which goes to the Champion at the end of each tournament — together with gifts of merchandise that may involve as many mushrooms as a *rikishi* can eat or a year's free supply of petrol — three other awards are made.

The most prestigious of these is the Technique Award (*Gino-sho*), which goes to the wrestler with the greatest technical prowess.

The Outstanding Performance Award (*Shukun-sho*) usually goes to a *rikishi* who has succeeded in beating one or more *yokozuna*.

And the Fighting Spirit Prize (*Kanto-sho*), which is given to the wrestler who has fought hard and won against the odds.

Mass production of souvenior handprints or *tegata*.

These prizes include cash and bonus increments, but they carry most weight with fan clubs and supporters who have been known to demonstrate their delight by showering favoured *rikishi* with fast cars and foreign trips.

All in all, middle-ranking young wrestlers in the top division can expect to earn more than £40,000 a year. While older and more successful fighters are likely to be in the six figure bracket. But the real money in sumo, as in other sports, goes to the really popular performers, who can expect to make huge amounts from personal appearances or television commercials.

Two money-spinners unique to sumo are the autograph parties where *rikishi* sign *tegata* — cards which bear their palm prints; and the final retirement ceremony where admirers each pay for the privilege of cutting a small lock from the wrestler's topknot.

Two *yokozuna* at a public function.

12 STABLES · HOW DO THEY LIVE?

Above: A novice warms up against the training pole.
Opposite
Above left: *Yokozuna* Chiyonofuji at ease in the traditional full-split position.
Above right: Young wrestlers being pressed into the painful position that gives experienced *sekitori* such suppleness.
Below left: Two heavyweights in training.
Below right: A wrestler bangs his head against the training post to harden it.

•

All wrestlers must belong to a stable or *heya*. And all but the most successful *rikishi*, who can afford their own accommodation, live in.

There are 39 *heya*, all based in Tokyo and most concentrated in the suburb of Ryogoku near the Kokugikan stadium where three of the six annual tournaments are held. Each of these stables is run by a master, who must be one of the 105 elders or *toshiyori* in the Japan Sumo Association. In addition to purchasing his title and traditional name, such an ex-wrestler must also find the funds to take over an existing *heya* from another stable master or, in exceptional circumstances, be given permission to start a new one. And from that moment on, he becomes the mentor, foster-father and nominal lord of a small, tightly knit and almost feudal family.

It is in his *heya* that a young wrestler learns the discipline of sumo. Skill and technique are learned later, with experience, but every aspect of stable life is dedicated to instilling obedience and a deep respect for tradition. The active life of a *rikishi* is short and, for the favoured few, can provide rich rewards, but it is never an easy option.

Most new recruits to sumo join straight from junior high school at the age of 15 or 16, usually as a result of recommendations from their local supporters' group or amateur sumo club. And, once accepted by a stable, they are offered nothing but the three necessities of life — food, clothing and shelter — in return for total loyalty and unquestioning obedience, with no days off.

For an apprentice, the sumo day begins at about 4.30 am when the dormitory is roused and set to work on an endless round of chores which begins even before training starts at dawn. The youngsters are the first into

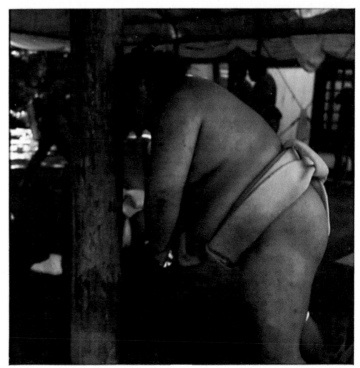

the stable's practice ring, where they loosen up with basic exercises such as *shiko* — high stamps with each leg in turn; *teppo* — slamming the open hands into a wooden pillar; and the painful *matawari* — a sort of sumo 'split' in which the legs are held out sideways at right angles to the body, while a trainer forces the seated novice's chest down to touch the ground.

Then come *moshiai* — a noisy elimination contest in the ring, with the winner of each bout staying in to nominate and take on his next eager opponent. This is usually followed by *sanban* — a long series of bouts against the same opponent, to test endurance and refine points of technique. Throughout all this, a coach and the stable master watch with rapt attention, making their presence felt with sharp words of instruction or an occasional slap with a bamboo stick or the handle of a broom. And, finally, ringwork ends with an exhausting exercise called *butsukari-geiko*, which involves running full tilt, again and again, into a more solid senior, who digs his heels in and allows himself either to be pushed back to the edge of the ring or throws the young assailant down in a way that teaches him how to fall.

Junior wrestlers offering water to a senior during practice.
Above right: Testing a bicycle to destruction.

As the morning training session or *keiko* progresses, the higher-ranking wrestlers drift in to take part and provide encouragement in the form of cuffs or slaps dished out apparently indiscriminately. These hard knocks are called *kawaigatte* — which literally means 'to treat with love and affection' – and are designed to make a novice angry and to give him the unique combination of acceptance and fighting spirit necessary to becoming a good *rikishi*.

After their two or three hour morning workout, the novices stand around, sweating and covered with dirt, ready to offer a towel or a drink of water to the senior to whom each has been assigned as a *tsukebito* or servant. And they dance such attendance until the practice session ends at about 11 am and the big men go off to have their baths. While they relax in the hot tubs, the juniors scurry around, still unwashed, preparing the morning meal, taking turns with the cooking and cleaning, serving, filling rice bowls and washing the dishes. And only after everyone else has finished eating and gone off to have a midday nap, can the young recruits sit down and finish what is left before going off to take their own baths.

Champion Konishiki
in the pink.

Small wonder that six out of every ten novices who join a stable end up running away in the first year.

Junior men in a stable don't get to sleep during the day. While their elders lie about putting on the pounds, the youngsters tidy up, do the laundry, clean the toilets, go shopping or run errands until it is time to prepare the evening meal for those seniors who are not out visiting schools, promoting good causes, dining with supporters or making guest appearances on television. In between the hard-working novices and the big men in social demand, are the fortunate middle-rankers, who have earned the right to be waited on without yet having to take on the responsibilities of being at the top. They can relax, watch television, have their hair done, play a little baseball or a card game, do a jigsaw puzzle or listen to their favourite pop music. They occupy a sort of limbo world, nourished and supported by the stable family, enjoying the fruits of communal life, making friends and absorbing the inheritance of sumo, while not having to do much more about it than maintain their rank by winning a requisite number of bouts at each tournament. Some wrestlers stick at this level throughout their sumo careers, going on (if they are lucky) to become cooks or trainers in the same stable after their retirement around the age of 30. In many ways, they are the lifeblood of sumo, vital to the system, but they — and everyone else in this traditional world — are in the service of the Champions, the men who go on to strive for perfection and win titles.

Success in sumo is independent of age or seniority. Rank transcends all

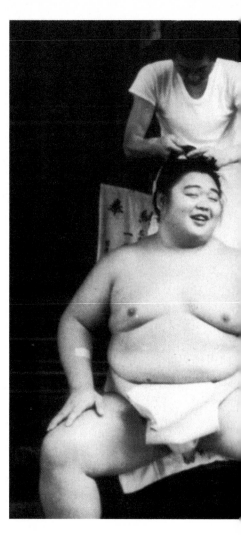

other factors in the pecking order and a stable is only as good as its highest ranking wrestlers — the *sekitori*. Promotion to the upper two Divisions changes everything in a fighter's life. He gets respect, a new hairstyle, a white training belt, a fancy silk fighting belt and, best of all, a salary. For the first time he has a little independence from the stable – a chance to buy his own meals, travel by taxi, and even to get out of the dormitory by renting an outside room or apartment.

But the rank also carries obligations, both financial and personal. A *sekitori* has to dress right, own several expensive ceremonial aprons, be in a position to give as well as receive gifts and, above all, behave in a dignified

manner on all occasions. He ceases to have any real private life. Every visit to a shop or restaurant becomes a public event. Every gesture, every word is scrutinized for extra significance. His friendships become the subject of endless gossip and his marriage an occasion for national rejoicing. As a leading player in Japan's national sport, he is an automatic celebrity, a star — and is expected to behave accordingly. It is then that he finds that it is only in his *heya*, his adopted home, that he can relax amongst fellow athletes — people who really know what it has cost him to get to the top.

Only one in every thousand recruits ever gets to be a *yokozuna*, but that one is very special indeed — more of a man in a million.

13 FOOD · WHAT DO THEY EAT?

*T*he secret of the sumo diet is a stew called *chanko-nabe*. *Chanko* is whatever is available. There are no set recipes. It usually consists of about a dozen ingredients, most of them fresh vegetables in season, plus poultry, pork or fish with a flavouring of sugar and soy. The vegetables are sliced thin enough to cook quickly and the meats are either reduced to bite-size pieces or minced and squeezed into small, rubbery balls. And everything is allowed to simmer in water, kelp soup or chicken stock for about fifteen minutes. A typical *chanko* may contain carrot, onion, cabbage, leek, spinach, beansprouts, mushroom, *tofu* and fermented bean paste in rice vinegar or *sake*. All the best ones stick to just one kind of meat — most often squid or white fish. The whole thing is brewed up as a one-pot stew which is nutritious, cheap, easy to make — and delicious.

There are popular *chanko* restaurants in Ryogoku, the sumo district of Tokyo, most of them run by ex-wrestlers. These tend to serve slightly re-fined and more varied versions of *chanko-nabe*, with a wide range of side dishes. But the real thing is the basic brew, cooked up in every stable every day in enormous metal pots as big as wash basins.

Cooking is usually done by the younger wrestlers on a roster basis, but those stables renowned for the quality of their *chanko* all have a profes-sional in charge of their kitchens. He may be the stable master himself, but more often is an old hand who never got promoted to the top two Divisions and laboured long enough in the lower ranks to become expert in such chores. The wise stable hangs on to such a treasure, keeping him on after retirement as a permanent cook, who shops himself for the best ingredients and keeps his kitchen crew busy turning out the vast quantities necessary to feed 30 or 40 ravenous and rapidly growing young wrestlers.

Chanko is not in itself overly fattening, but the amount eaten is enormous, served with unlimited bowls of rice, and washed down with ample beer and *sake*. And all meals are followed by mandatory naps, which seem to help to convert the calories into substantial flesh. In between meals, all *rikishi* are very partial to noodles, and the younger ones, once they can afford to, become regular and welcome visitors to local fried chicken, hamburger and other fast food stores. Many are, in addition, prodigious drinkers with a capacity for alcohol which leaves their fans and supporters literally staggering.

Most evenings, the stable kitchens are quiet, with the older wrestlers all out on social rounds. The popular ones are almost 'male geisha', invited to add prestige to dinner parties, where they always eat well, sometimes sing for their supper and inevitably end up being photographed with everyone in the room. For this service, they routinely receive a discreet and untaxable gift of around £500 in cash, usually described as *kuruma-dai* or 'car-fare'. A title-holder usually gets somewhat more and a new Champion is fêted so lavishly that it is almost impossible for him to do well in any tournament coming directly after his promotion.

On the evening of *senshuraku*, the final day of each tournament, there is a stable party organized by the *koenkai* or supporters' club, which consists of up to 500 fee-paying members. Ordinary supporters get two tickets for each *basho* in their home town and the chance to mingle with their favourite wrestlers over a celebratory drink. Special supporters, who pay heavily for the privilege, are invited to accompany all the stable retinue on their annual visit to a hill shrine and hot spring. But the elite of sumo fans are fanatical patrons known as *tanimachi* — after a doctor who once lived on a street of that name in Osaka and treated all wrestlers free of charge. These wealthy men are the only ones who dare to, or can afford to, entertain twenty-stone guests to dinner on a regular basis. Feeding one is an endeavour not to be taken lightly.

14 RETIREMENT · IS THERE LIFE AFTER SUMO?

Above: Wakashimazu, one of the lighter top-rank wrestlers, poses with an admirer's baby shortly before his retirement.
Opposite: Hawaiian-born Takamiyama's tearful departure from active wrestling in 1985. He is now Master of Azumazeki stable.

*S*umo is tough and very few *rikishi* remain active until the age of 40. Most retire in their early 30s.

Retirement is marked by an emotional ceremony called *danpatsu-shiki* which involves cutting off the *rikishi's* distinctive topknot. The man himself sits in a chair on the *dohyo* while hundreds of patrons, friends and fans file by and take turns to snip at his top-knot. The last strands are ceremonially cut by his own stable-master with a pair of long brass scissors.

High-ranking *rikishi* nearly always stay in the business — either as stable-masters in their own right (if they can afford to buy the necessary stock), or as coaches and administrators. A few go into business on their own, some as restaurateurs, and one or two have become successful pop stars. But all lose most of their bulk in a matter of months, looking before long like large but otherwise quite ordinary people.

A few *rikishi* pay the price for carrying that extra weight over their active years in weakened hearts and a tendency toward diabetes. And some bear the marks of all athletes in injuries to knees and tendons. But most go on, reduced in size, to lead long and happy lives. A survey of 100 top wrestlers active in the early part of the Showa period (beginning in 1926) shows that, contrary to rumour, the average age at death was 64 — despite the fact that five of the fatalities were early ones occasioned by the occupational hazard of being poisoned by *fugu*, a fish dish very popular with sumo wrestlers.

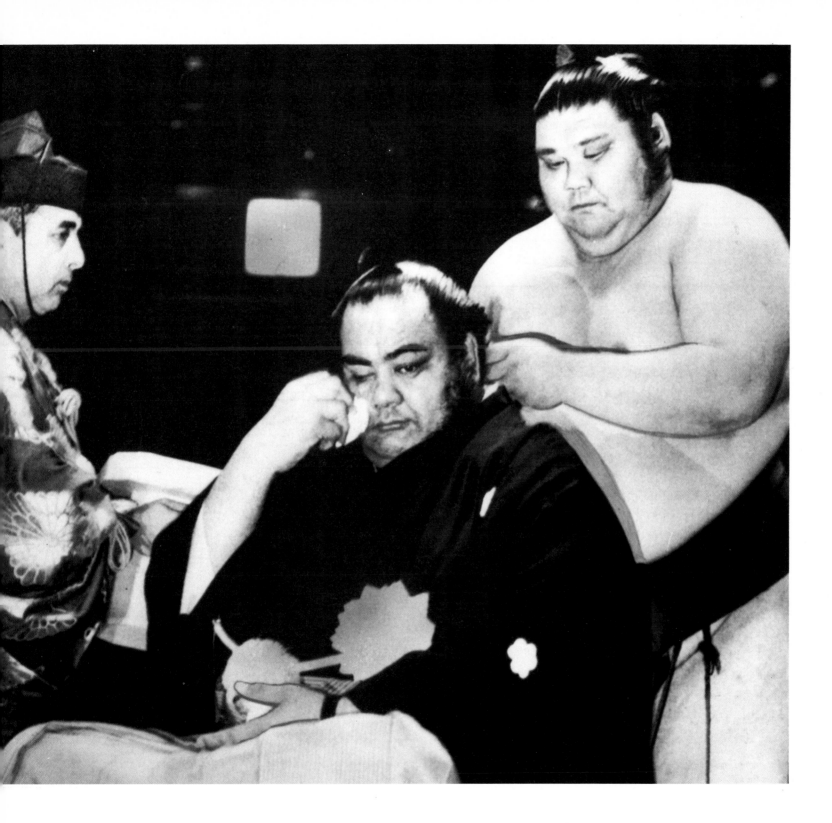

15 NAMES · WHAT DO THEY MEAN?

Opposite: Koji Kitao, who became *yokozuna* Futahaguro.

•

*T*hose who practise sumo start off with perfectly ordinary Japanese names like Akimoto, Nakayama and Tanaka.

A few, whose surnames are unusual and already have a good sound — such as Itai or Kurama — keep them. A recent *yokozuna* was persuaded only with difficulty that it was necessary at his exalted rank to change from his family name of Kitao to something more formal. He became Futa-haguro, which means 'two mountains'.

Most wrestlers above a certain level adopt a traditional sumo name or *shikona*. These are always poetic and frequently include the elements *hana* (flower), *yama* (mountain), *kaze* (wind), *koto* (lute), *tama* (jewel), *waka* (young) and *umi* (sea). Dewanohana therefore means 'flower of the north'. Tamaryu is 'the jewelled dragon'. Hananoumi is 'lake or sea of flowers'. Wakashimazu is 'the young warlord'. Asashio is 'the morning tide'. And Daijuyama 'the big happy mountain'.

No two fighters may have the same name, and none get to choose for themselves. Most stables have their own traditional *shikona*. Every member of the Sadogatake Beya, for instance, has a name which begins with Koto. Anyone called Dewa- will belong to Dewanoumi Beya, and the prefix Tatsu- is the mark of a wrestler from the stable of Tatsunami. Stable masters often choose to honour a particularly promising young *rikishi* with their own fighting names.

On retirement, wrestlers either go back to their family names or, to create even further confusion, become stable-masters and have to adopt yet another title. The Hawaiian Jesse Kuhaulua, for instance, who broke sumo records as Takamiyama, is now Azumazeki — master of his own stable.

1. Chiyonofuji

'The Wolf'

Yokozuna of Kokonoe Stable. Age 34. 6 ft. 265 lbs (18 stone 13). His fighting name literally means 'A Thousand Generations of Fuji' – and by early 1990 he will have fought a thousand bouts in the top division and won well over seven hundred of these, serving as grand champion for 9 years and winning half the tournaments in which he has taken part. He remains one of the lightest fighters, but has such power and skill that he is still the hardest man to beat.

*I*t remains as difficult as ever to predict who will be winning the big prizes in Sumo in the future, but these 24 of the 38 wrestlers currently fighting in the top division seem likely to dominate Sumo in the coming year.

2. Hokutoumi

'The Bulldog'

Yokozuna, also of Kokonoe Stable. Age 26. 5 ft 11. 313 lbs (22 stone 5). His name derives from the characters for 'North', 'Victory' and 'Sea', because like stable-mate Chiyonofuji he comes from the northern island of Hokkaido. Since promotion in 1987, he has proved a solid and powerful grand champion, difficult to resist when he muscles his way inside an opponent's guard and applies his favourite right hand thrust to the throat.

3. Onokuni

'The Giant Panda'

Yokozuna of Hanaregoma Stable. Age 27. 6 ft 2. 461 lbs (32 stone 13). Name means 'Big Country', and he is still the largest Japanese-born Sumo wrestler. Since his promotion to the top in 1987, he has been somewhat erratic. On a good day he looks unbeatable, but sometimes he seems ponderous and slow. His long-term future must be in doubt unless he can exercise more aggression and avoid lapses in concentration.

5. Hokutenyu
'The Polar Bear'

Ozeki of the Mihogaseki Stable. Age 29. 6 ft. 318 lbs (22 stone 10). The 'Northern Gift from Heaven' is another Hokkaido man with all the talents necessary to make it to the top. He already has two titles and has served six good years on the second rung, but seems to lack the spark, spirit and consistency necessary to make it all the way. The next year will be crucial for him.

▲ 4. Asahifuji
'The Sea Slug'

Ozeki of Oshima Stable. Age 29. 6 ft 2. 320 lbs (22 stone 12). The 'Rising Sun of Fuji' looked like becoming a *yokozuna* in 1988, but he fell just short of the necessary qualification. He only just failed again in 1989, losing a vital playoff to Hokutoumi in May, and now has to prove himself all over again in his thirtieth year. He has the skill and flashes of the right spirit, but sometimes seems a little bored, as though he would rather be on his favourite trout stream.

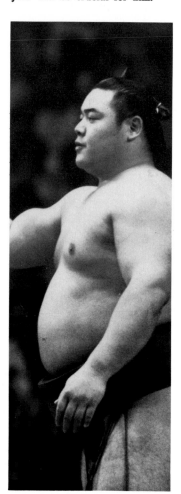

6. Konishiki
'The Dump Truck'

Ozeki of Takasago Stable. Age 26. 6 ft 2. 498 lbs (35 stone 8). This Hawaiian is still the biggest thing in Sumo, but is now about 50 lbs below the top weight he reached in 1987. He has recurrent trouble with his knees and seems unlikely now ever to make it to *yokozuna*. There have been moments recently when he seemed on the brink of demotion, but on good days when he can summon up his full fighting spirit and keep his balance, he remains very difficult to beat. The fighting name is ironic, meaning 'Little Trophy or Banner'.

7. Kotogaume
'The Plum'

Sadogatake Stable. Age 26. 5 ft 11. 392 lbs (28 stone). Name derives from *koto* – a traditional stringed instrument – and 'Flowering Plum'. After four years in the top division, he seems to be coming into his own, reaching the rank of *sekiwake*. He is powerful and solid, a little erratic on occasion, but a strong candidate for possible promotion to *ozeki*.

8. Tochinowaka
'The Mighty Oak'

Kasugano Stable. Age 27. 6 ft 3. 322 lbs (23 stone). The 'Great Tree' of Wakayama Prefecture. Bounces up and down the ranks – one of eight current wrestlers who reach the rank of *sekiwake* whenever they can get everything together and avoid injury. Has the power to produce occasional upsets over the champions and could still earn promotion to *ozeki*.

9. Mitoizumi
'The Salt Shaker'

Takasago Stable. Age 27. 6 ft 4. 392 lbs (28 stone). Name means 'Spring' or 'Fountain' from the place called Mito. A pale green belt and a last prodigious throw of salt have become the trademarks of this genial and ebullient wrestler, who keeps upsetting the champions. If he were not so injury prone, he would by now be an *ozeki*. Always worth watching.

◀ 10. Akinoshima
'The Killer Whale'

Fujishima Stable. Age 22. 5 ft 9. 287 lbs (20 stone 7). This tough young wrestler, named for an island in the Prefecture of Hiroshima, is one of the bright young hopes of Sumo. He burst into the top division in 1988 and, despite his small size, has been the scourge of the big men ever since. He shows a maturity and presence on the *dohyo* which are remarkable for anyone his age. With a little more experience, he could rise right to the top.

11. Kirishima
'The Fog'

Izutsu Stable. Age 30. 6 ft 2. 256 lbs (18 stone 4). One of the 'Famous Five' fighters from this stable now in the top division – three of whom have made it to the rank of *sekiwake*. 'The Fog' (his name means 'Foggy Island') has thickened in the last year, putting on a lot of muscle and looking very good and dangerous. A master of the difficult *utchari* technique, he could yet be promoted to the top ranks.

12. Sakahoko
'The Spear'

Izutsu Stable. Age 28. 5 ft 11. 280 lbs (20 stone). The name means 'Reverse or Backward Spear'. Despite his soft appearance, he is one of the most canny fighters, very quick on his feet and just as effective going backwards as coming forward. Is a regular on the rank of *sekiwake*, but unlikely perhaps to go any higher. His stable-master father once held the same rank.

13. Terao
'The Typhoon'

Izutsu Stable. Age 26. 6 ft 1. 247 lbs (17 stone 9). Younger brother to Sakahoko. Fights under his late mother's maiden name. Has, like Kirishima, been building strength in weight training and turning all his weight into formidable muscle. One of the most spirited fighters. A real crowd pleaser who never gives up and could even overtake his brother in the race for promotion to *ozeki*.

14. Masurao ▶
'The Warrior'

Oshiogawa Stable. Age 28. 6 ft 2. 269 lbs (19 stone 3). A brave and spirited fighter with the look of a samurai warrior, who was injured in 1988 and fell to the second division, but is now fighting his way back to the top. Has been ranked as *sekiwake* and could reach that level again soon.

17. Hananokuni

'Flower Power'

Hanaregoma Stable. Age 30. 6 ft 1. 313 lbs (22 stone 5). One of the strongest men in Sumo, who can spring surprises even on the champions. Hovers near the top of the senior ranks, but unlikely because of his age to go much higher. Name means 'Land of Flowers'.

15. Jingaku

'The Fort'

Izutsu Stable. Age 29. 6 ft 2. 313 lbs (22 stone 5). Another of the 'Famous Five'. Has reached *komusubi* and could do so again, but despite his large size seems to lack the power and consistency to do really well. His name derives from the characters for 'Military Base on a Mountain'.

16. Fujinoshin

'The Truth'

Kokonoe Stable. Age 29. 5 ft 11. 315 lbs (22 stone 7). A powerful fighter with the considerable advantage of training every day with Chiyonofuji and Hokutoumi, yet seems to lack the skill necessary to do really well. Hovering near the top of the senior ranks. Name means the 'True Mount Fuji'.

18. Kyokudozan
'Sundance'

Oshima Stable. Age 25. 5 ft 11. 218 lbs (15 stone 8). The lightest man in the top division, with wonderful fighting spirit and tenacity. Almost as great a crowd pleaser as Terao, but even more urgently needs extra weight if he is to get anywhere near the top. His name derives from the characters for 'Morning Sun' and 'Mountain Path'.

19. Ryogoku
'Local Hero'

Dewanoumi Stable. Age 27. 6 ft 1. 381 lbs (27 stone 3). A powerful wrestler, named after the Sumo district of Tokyo, who has been as high as *komusubi*, but needs greater technical skill if he is to get back to the upper ranks.

20. Kushimaumi ▶
'Rising Star'

Dewanoumi Stable. Age 24. 6 ft 2. 366 lbs (26 stone 2). A very recent newcomer to the top division, but this stable mate of Ryogoku has such awesome strength and technique that he is already being spoken of as a possible candidate for *ozeki*.

21. Misugisato
'The Cedar'

Futagoyama Stable. Age 27. 6 ft 1. 298 lbs (21 stone 4). Late in coming to the top division, he is still young enough to make his mark. Very versatile and skillful. His name derives from the characters for 'Three Cedars' and 'Village'.

24. Kotoinazuma
'Lightning'

Sadogatake Stable. Age 27. 5 ft 11. 282 lbs (20 stone 2). Another of the four 'Koto's' – all from this stable – this one's name includes the character for 'Lightning'. He is a fighter of enormous spirit who is becoming a well-known 'elevator *rikishi*' – one of those who rise and fall through the ranks at irregular intervals.

22. Enazakura
'The Cherry'

Oshiogawa Stable. Age 29. 5 ft 11. 295 lbs (21 stone 1). Another latecomer, but a skillful fighter who could with more consistency, get near the top ranks. Name means the 'Flowering Cherry Tree'.

23. Kotonishiki
'The Lute'

Sadogatake Stable. Age 21. 5 ft 9. 297 lbs (20 stone 7). The youngest fighter in the top division and one of the lightest. Very strong and not unlike Akinoshima in his build and his capacity to surprise. The characters in his name mean 'Lute' and 'Trophy'.

17 WHAT'S HAPPENING? SUMO UPDATE

For Sumo fans, 1988 was the Year of the Wolf. Chiyonofuji won four of the six *basho*, moving into second place on the all-time list of *yusho* winners behind the great Taiho who dominated the sport in the 1960s. He also racked up an astonishing winning streak of 45 bouts in a row, falling finally to *yokozuna* Onokuni in the last bout of the last day of the final tournament of the year.

That *basho* in Kyushu, which the Wolf won for the eighth successive year, also proved to be the last of the Showa Era. Emperor Hirohito, Sumo's patron and most influential follower, died the following month.

The New Year and the new era began with a Kokonoe see-saw. The fact that two of the three reigning *yokozuna* come from Kokonoe Stable gives both of them an enormous advantage over everyone else. No stable mates may meet on the *dohyo* except in the rare case of a playoff between them on the final day – so while other high-ranking wrestlers have to fight all three grand champions during the course of a tournament, the 'Wolf' and the 'Bulldog' need only deal with 'Giant Panda' Onokuni.

Hokutoumi sat out the last three tournaments in 1988 with a back injury, but he bounced back into action in January with a splendid win. In March, it was Chiyonofuji's turn again and he stormed through the tournament, trouncing Onokuni on the 14th day, but in the process of upending the 32-stone 'Panda', the Master dislocated his right shoulder. He missed the final day, but won the title anyway, bringing his career total to 27 *yusho*.

With the Wolf missing again from the pack in May, Hokutoumi took the title, but not without an epic struggle against *ozeki* Asahifuji. The 'Sea Slug'

Konishiki losing to Hananokuni

Hokutenyu losing to Terao

and the 'Bulldog' met in a playoff on the final day, when Hokutoumi yet again destroyed the unfortunate *ozeki*'s chance of promotion to *yokozuna*.

May was an historic *basho*. Both the 'Wolf' and the 'Bulldog' were well and ended up on the final day with a tie that forced them into the first playoff this century between *yokozuna* from the same stable. Both men looked uneasy at the prospect, meeting for the first time ever in open competition, but it was the Boss who took the initiative and his 28th tournament title.

March 1989 was the last appearance of 'Big Boy' Asashio, whose retirement left Sumo with just three other *ozeki* to back up the reigning *yokozuna*. There have been no promotions to either rank since 1987, but with eight senior wrestlers taking it in turns to occupy the four positions in the supporting ranks of *sekiwake* and *komusubi*, the scene seems set for one or two of these Young Turks to show the sort of consistency and momentum the Sumo Association requires for promotion to the top.

Sakahoko is the spearhead of the group, but he seems content to be a

Ryogoku losing to Chiyonofuji

perennial junior champion. His younger brother 'Typhoon' Terao is becoming bigger and stronger with each *basho*, but may well be too fiery to settle into the more rigorous demands of championship. The best candidates for promotion look like 'Salt Shaker' Mitoizumi and the 'Mighty Oak' Tochinowaka, but both have old injuries and the race may go in the end to newcomer Akinoshima who, despite his relatively small size, has the sort of chunky persistence of which true champions are made.

One of the most interesting trends in recent months has been the progress of several lightweights in the Chiyonofuji mould. Kirishima at 256 pounds, Terao at 247, Masurao at 269 and Kyokudozan at just 218 pounds, are all demonstrating that speed and fighting spirit can succeed against the heavy brigade. None of them may ever reach the 'Wolf's' lofty level, but they bring an excitement and sparkle to Sumo which has been lacking for a while.

'Dumptruck' Konishiki remains the highest-ranking foreigner in Sumo. There are 19 other *gaijin* scattered through the ranks, including three in the third division who may soon be seen in silk *mawashi*. But our attention in Britain is going to be focussed in the next few years on the first-ever English *rikishi*, who joined Azumazeki Stable in June 1989. Nathan Strange is due to make his debut on the *dohyo* in September as Hidenokuni – the 'Winning Countryman of England'. We hope he lasts long enough and does well enough to return to London in triumph as a junior member of the touring party destined for a huge welcome here in October 1991.

18 GLOSSARY · SUMO TERMS

Banzuke
List of rankings.

Basho
Sumo tournament.

Bintsuke
Hair oil.

Butsukari-geiko
Pushing exercise.

Chankonabe
High protein diet.

Chaya
Sumo teashop.

Chon-mage
Topknot worn by *rikishi*.

Danpatsu-shiki
Hair-cutting ceremony.

Deshi
Apprentice wrestler.

Dohyo
Sumo ring.

Dohyo-iri
Ring-entering ceremony.

Dohyo-matsuri
Ring-dedication ceremony.

Gyoji
Referee.

Hataki-komi
'Slap down' technique.

Heya (beya)
Sumo stable.

Hidari
Left hander.

Hikkake
'Pulling' technique.

Jinku
Sumo song.

Jonidan
Second Division from the bottom.

Jonokuchi
First step from the bottom.

Jungyo
Exhibition tour of provinces.

Juryo
Second Division from the top.

Kachi-koshi
Majority of wins — score of 8–7 or better.

Kanto-sho
Fighting Spirit Prize.

Kawaigatte
Roughing-up experienced by new recruits to a stable.

Keiko
Practice or training.

Ketaguir
'Leg sweep' technique.

Kimarite
Sumo techniques.

Kokugikan
Stadium in Tokyo.

Kote-nage
'Forearm throw' technique.

Komusubi
Junior Champion (2nd class).

Kyokai
Japan Sumo Association.

Maegashira
Senior wrestler of top Division.

Make-koshi
Majority of losses — score of 7–8 or worse.

Makunouchi
Top Division.

Makushita
Third highest Division.

Masuzeki
Ringside boxes.

Matawari
Sumo split exercise in which chest is pressed to the ground.

Mawashi
Loincloth belt.

Migi
Right hander.

Moro Zashi
Both hands on the belt.

Moshiai
An elimination contest in training.

O icho mage
Hairstyle of top division wrestler.

Okuri dashi
'Push out from behind' technique.

Oshi dashi
'Push out' technique.

Oshi taoshi
'Push down' technique.

Oshi zumo
'Pushing' technique.

Oyakata
Elder of the Association.

Ozeki
Champion.

Rikishi
All ranks of wrestlers.

Sagari
String belt.

Sanban
Training bouts against a single opponent.

Sandanme
Third Division from the bottom.

Sanyaku
Three top ranks below *yokozuna*.

Sekitori
Wrestlers of two top Divisions.

Sekiwake
Junior Champion (1st class).

Senshuraku
Final day of tournament.

Shiko
Exercise in which one foot is raised high and stamped down hard.

Shikona
Sumo name.

Shimpan
Ring side judge.

Shitate-nage
'Inner arm throw' technique.

Shukun-sho
Outstanding Performance Award.

Soto-gake
'Outer leg trip' technique.

Sumotori
Wrestlers below the top two Divisions.

Tachi-ai
Initial charge.

Tegata
Palm print.

Teppo
Exercise involving open-handed slaps against a wooden pole.

Tokoyama
Sumo hairdresser.

Toshiyori
One of 105 sumo elders.

Tsukebito
Attendant.

Tsuki dashi
'Thrust out' technique.

Tsuki otoshi
'Thrust over' technique.

Tsuki taoshi
'Thrust down' technique.

Tsuna
Ceremonial rope belt of *yokozuna*.

Tsuppari
'Slapping' technique.

Tsuri dashi
'Lift out' technique.

Tsuri otoshi
'Lift down' technique.

Tsuyu-harai
'Dew Sweeper' to a *yokozuna*.

Uchi-gake
'Inner leg trip' technique.

Utchari
'Throw down at edge of ring' technique.

Uwate-nage
'Outerarm throw' technique.

Yobidashi
Announcer.

Yorikiri
'Force out' technique.

Yori Taoshi
'Force out and down' technique.

Yotsu-zumo
'Grappling' techniques.

Yumitori-shiki
Bow twirling ceremony.

Yusho
Tournament championship.

Zensho yusho
Perfect victory 15—0.

Pronunciation is fairly simple. All syllables are given equal emphasis and the vowels sound as follows:

a in b*a*r
e in b*e*d
i in b*i*n
o in b*o*re
u in b*oo*k.

FURTHER INFORMATION

*T*he best way to learn about sumo is to keep on watching. We hope that with the help of this simple Guide you will be able to pick up some of the finer points and come to appreciate the subtlety and beauty of this traditional art.

And if you want more background information, we suggest:-

Benson, W. & Sackett, J. *Rikishi: The Men of Sumo*, (1986).
Cuyler, P. L. *Sumo: From Rite to Sport*, (1979).
Kenrick, D. *The Book of Sumo: Sport, Spectacle and Ritual*, (1969).
All published by Weatherhill in New York.

And, for up-to-the-moment news:
Sumo World — an English language magazine published six times a year by Andy Adams, c/o Foreign Press Club, Yurakucho Denki Building, 1-7-1 Yurakucho, Chiyoda-ku, Tokyo.
Subscription at the time of going to press is US$28.00 (about £17) per annum.

Photographic Credits:

The publishers would like to thank the following for supplying and giving their permission to reproduce the photographs:
Gerry Toff, Tokyo: frontispiece, pages 6, 8 (right), 14, 17 (both), 21 (right, all three), 22, 23, 24, 25, 28 (three), 30, 31 (below), 32, 33, 34, 35, 36, 39, 40, 45, 47 (above), 49, 51 (left), 52 (left), 54, 58, 64, 67 (both), 68, 69 (all four), 70 (both), 71, 72, 73, 78, 80, 82–94 (all photos)
Same Two Inc.: pages 8 (left), 10, 15, 19, 21 (left), 29, 31 (above), 37 (right), 38 (both), 41 (both), 42, 43 (both), 46, 47 (below), 50, 51 (below and right), 52 (right), 57, 59, 60, 62–63, 74–75
Frank Spooner Pictures: page 53
Popperfoto: pages 9, 37 (left), 79
Allsport: pages 26–27

And thanks to Mike Milne of Cheerleader for supplying the *banzuke* pictured on page 16 and for his valuable help and advice throughout.